Playtime FUN

The CRAYON SPINE ® is a registered trademark
of Playmore Inc., Publishers and Waldman Publishing Corp.

Published by Playmore Inc., Publishers and Waldman Publishing Corp.,
New York, New York

Copyright © MM Playmore Inc., Publishers and Waldman Publishing Corp.,
New York, New York

Printed in Canada

The Penguin Twins

Penny and Peter Penguin are twins, and they're on their way to an ice skating contest.

"Did you pack everything you'll need?"
asks Mrs. Penguin.

Scrambled Pictures

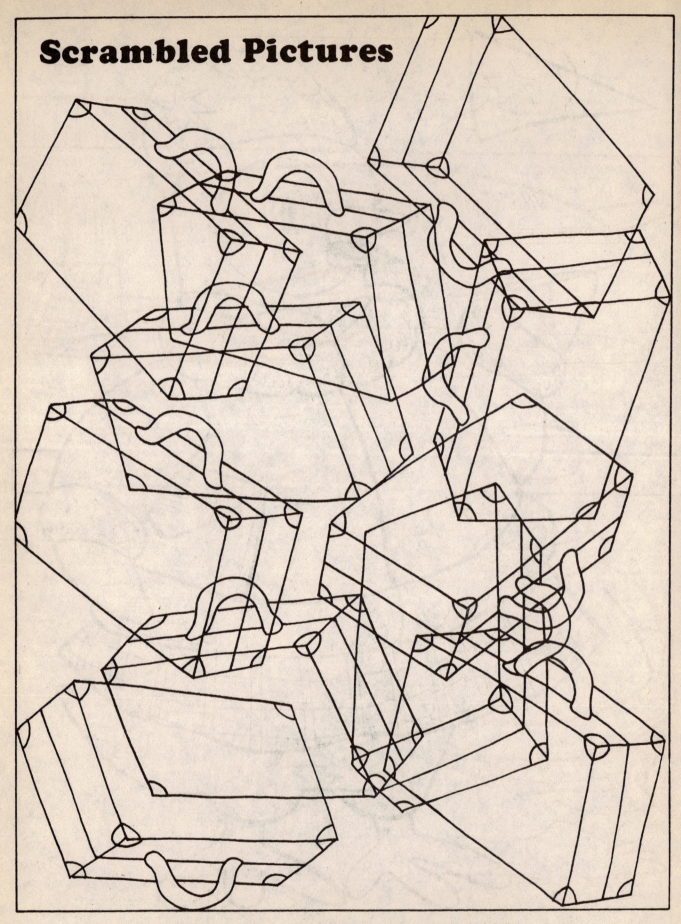

Can you count how many suitcases the penguin twins
are taking with them?

"Goodbye, Mom!"

The penguins arrive at the village . . .

. . . where they meet other contestants.

Betsy Bear will be in the ice skating contest too.

"Hello."

The twins take a walk and meet a skier along the way.

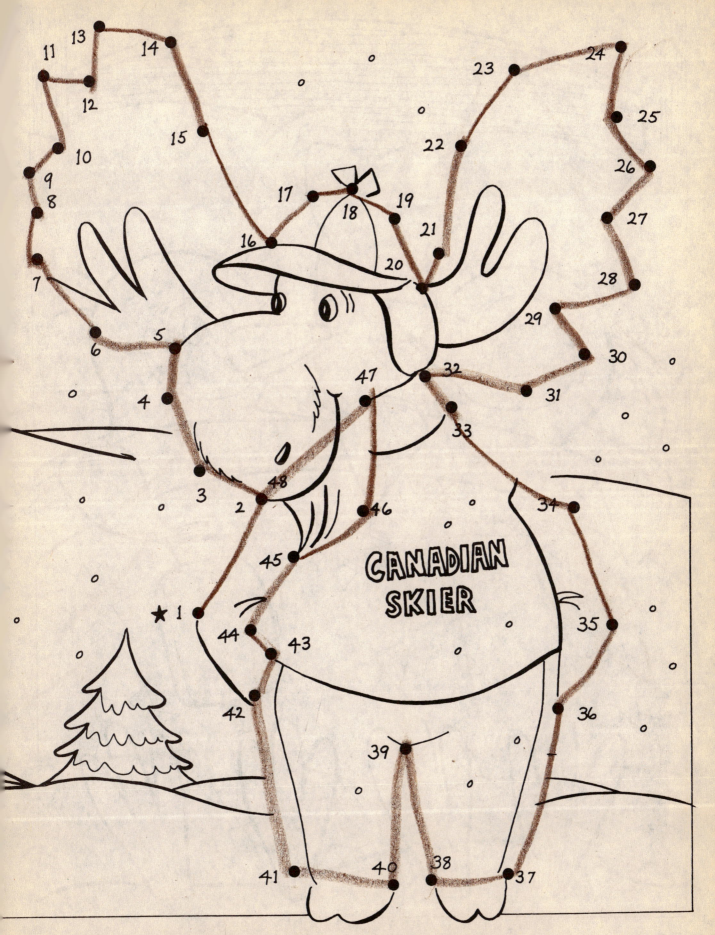

Connect the Dots to see who the twins met.

"We should get a good night's sleep.
Tomorrow is the big day."

The next morning, Penny and Peter dress up
in their skating costumes.

"There's Danny Dog skiing down the slope.
Do you think he'll win the skiing contest?"

Downhill Racer

Trace a path for Danny to show him
the way down the ski slope.

Color by Number

See Marty Moose on his skis.

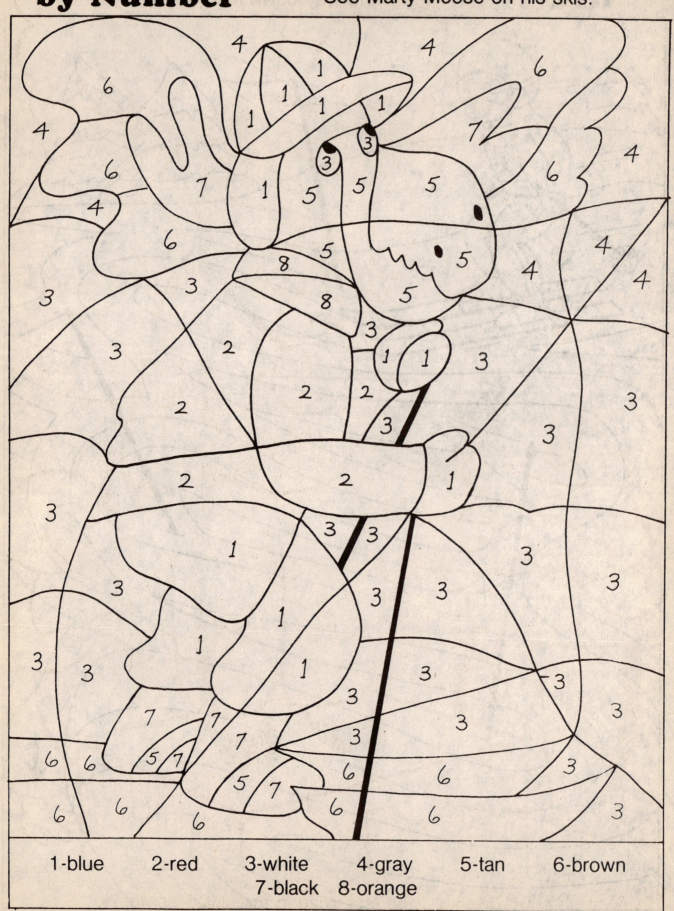

1-blue   2-red   3-white   4-gray   5-tan   6-brown
7-black   8-orange

Marty Moose wins first prize in the skiing contest!

It's Betsy Bear's turn on the ice.

"She's very good!"

"You were wonderful, Betsy."

"Now, from the South Pole—the Penguin Twins!"

Spin!

Twirl!

A Figure Skating Maze . . .

Help the twins skate through the rink . . .

... To Win First Prize!

... Trace the correct path for them through the maze.

"Bravo! Bravo!"

It's time for the judges to select
the ice skating champion.

It's a tie—the Penguin Twins and Betsy Bear
all win first prize!

The judges are very pleased.

Ice Skate Twins

Can you find a matching pair of ice skates?

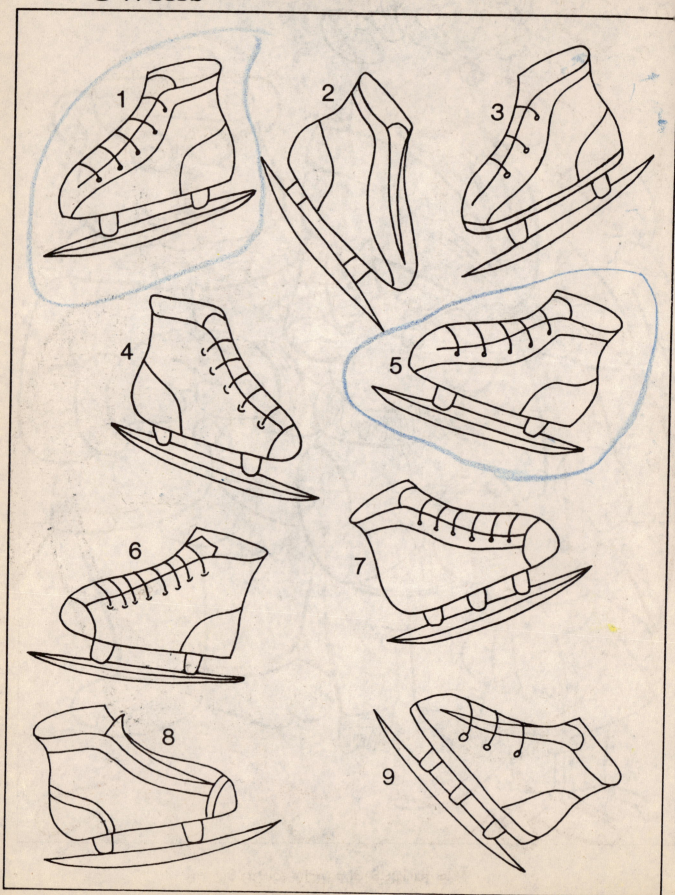

The twins are ready to go home.

AIRPORT

Mother Penguin meets them at the airport.
"We won first prize, Mom!"

A Day at the South Pole

The next day, the twins decide to go out and play.

"Look, over there. That's a good place
to build an ice castle!"

"The ice is really slippery!"

"We are lucky we know how to swim."

Find and Color

Find 4 swimming penguins and color them blue.

Peter and Penny gather ice blocks
for their castle . . .

. . . and the building begins.

"It's beautiful! If it weren't so cold,
we could plant flowers."

Penguin Mystery Word

Which are the penguins' favorite flowers?

In the squares going down from each picture, fill in the name of that picture. Then fill in the blank squares going across to find the answer to the question.

Now it's time for some fishing!

Tangled Lines

Trace a path along each fishing line to see which fish
each twin caught. Then color the picture.

"What a nice day we had today."

PENGUIN TWINS

Penguins live at the South Pole. Can you find the two penguins that look alike?

COLOR BY NUMBER

South Pole Penguin

1-blue   2-yellow   3-pink   4-violet

5-white   6-black

FOLLOW THE DOTS

See who likes to lead a Royal Parade!

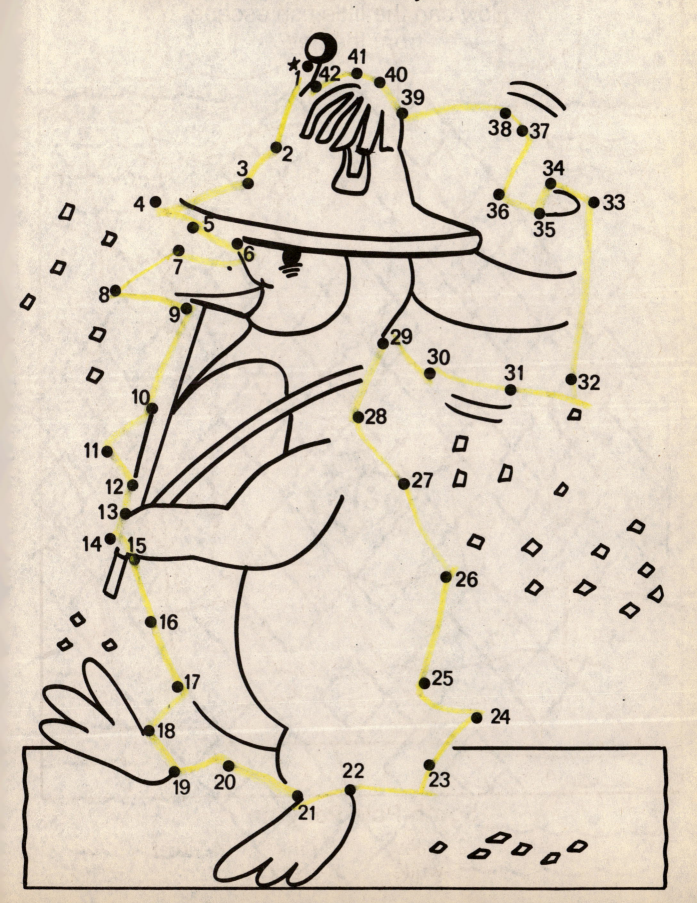

WRIGGLING FREE

How can the little fish escape
from the net?

FIND AND COUNT

Rick has caught a fish.
How many more fish can you
find hidden in the ocean?

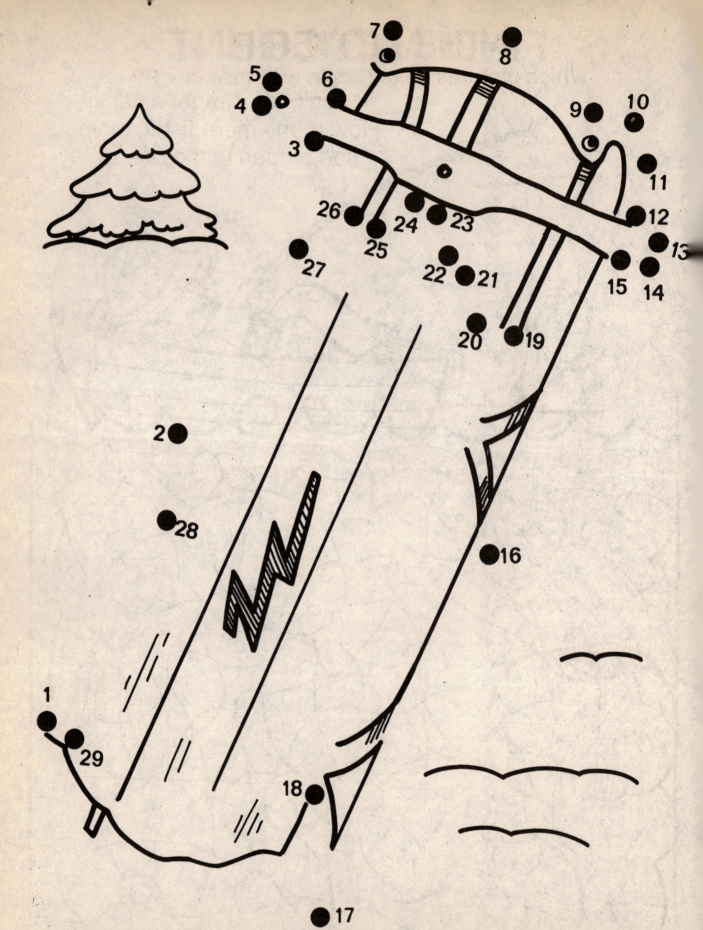

FOLLOW THE DOTS to see something fun to play with in the snow.

THE LETTER P
Which pictures below begin with the letter P?

A FISHING TRIP

Can you find the pictures below in the
same order in the squares?
You must look up, down, and across.

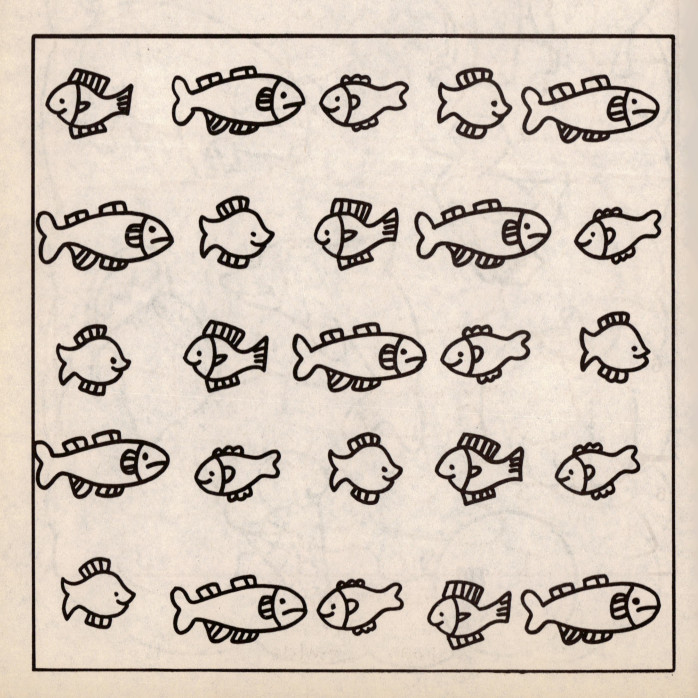

COLOR BY NUMBER

Eskimo Boy

1-black   2-blue   3-brown   4-orange
5-green   6-white

A Fun Day at the Farm

As the sun comes up the rooster crows . . .

. . . and wakes up everyone on the farm.
It's time to get up.

A new day on the farm is about to begin.

Farmer Frank and his wife start off the
day with a good breakfast.

Now Farmer Frank is ready to do his farm chores.

There's always so much to do on the farm.

Farmer Frank collects all the eggs . . .

. . . from his hens in the chicken coop.

The chickens wake up and walk around
outside the coop.

One chicken eats some seeds, while
another spreads its wings.

In the barnyard, the little chicks come out . . .

. . . to greet the new day.

In the barn, Farmer Frank milks one
of his cows.

After Farmer Frank milks the cow, he
will milk the goat.

Four goats are outside behind the barn.

Two of the goats are babies. Baby goats
like to play.

Farmer Frank's peacock spreads his
beautiful tail . . .

. . . while the turkey says, "Gobble, gobble, gobble."

A flock of sheep roam through the grass.

Here is a male sheep. A male sheep
is called a ram.

A horse eats some grass, while her two
young babies stay close by.

Baby horses are called foals.

This farm horse pulls a wagon full of hay.

Farmer Frank stores the hay in the barn.
Horses like to eat hay!

While the farmer plows his fields . . .

. . . two horses have fun running through
the meadow.

Donkeys are good farm animals. They can carry
heavy loads on their backs . . .

. . . . but sometimes they can be very stubborn!

Farmer Frank has a small pond behind
his house . . .

. . . and this is where the geese like
to stay during the day.

Hop, hop, hop go the rabbits.

Rabbits make their home in a hutch.

It's time to feed the pigs.

The pigs come running from all directions when they
see their food. How they love to eat!

Out by the hen house . . .

. . . sits the farm dog, Rover. He helps Farmer Frank
take care of the animals.

A busy day on the farm has come to an end, and Farmer Frank says good-night to all the farm animals.

FOLLOW THE DOTS

See who's making breakfast for
these little chicks!

FOLLOW THE DOTS

See who's having a vegetable snack!

FOLLOW THE DOTS

See who likes fishing!

FOLLOW THE DOTS

See a nice way to spend the day!

FOLLOW THE DOTS

See a sunny morning on the farm!

FOLLOW THE DOTS

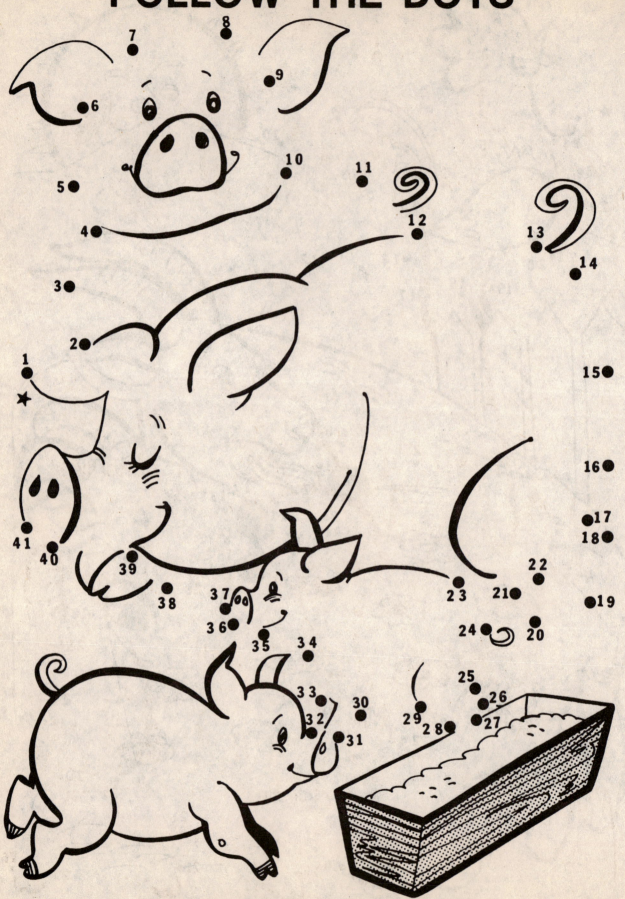

See this little pig's happy family!

FOLLOW THE DOTS

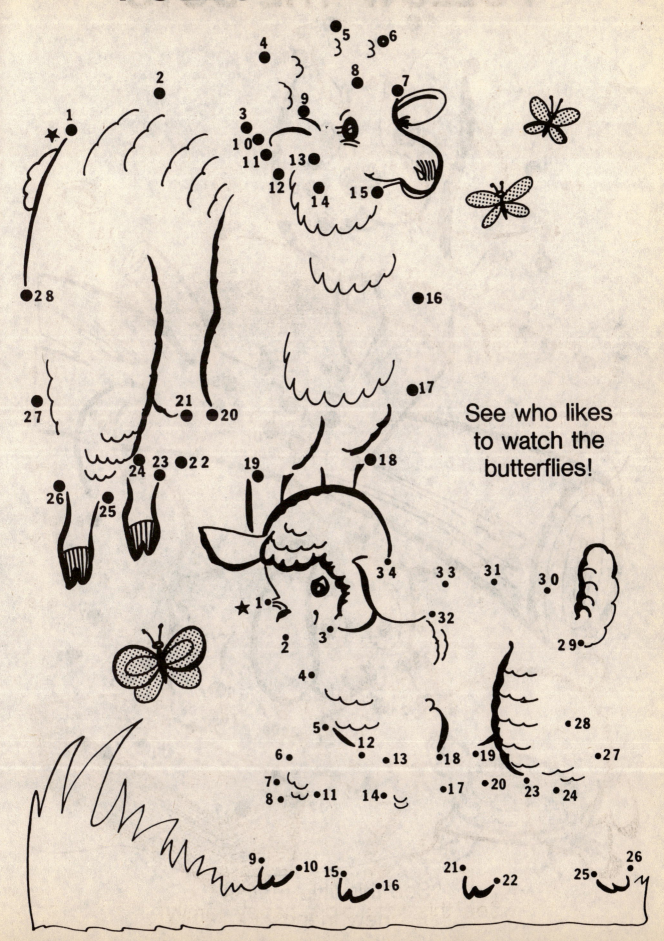

See who likes to watch the butterflies!

FOLLOW THE DOTS

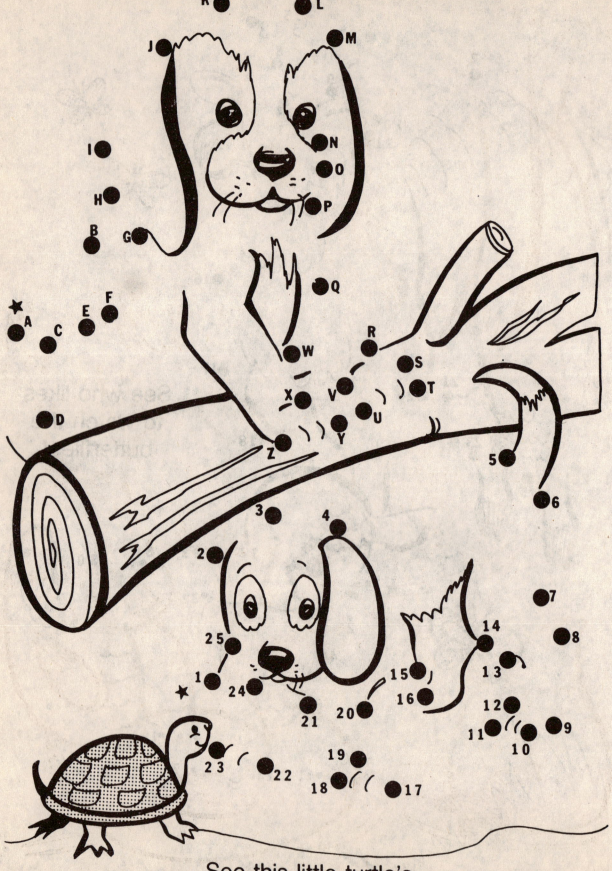

See this little turtle's
new friends!

FOLLOW THE DOTS

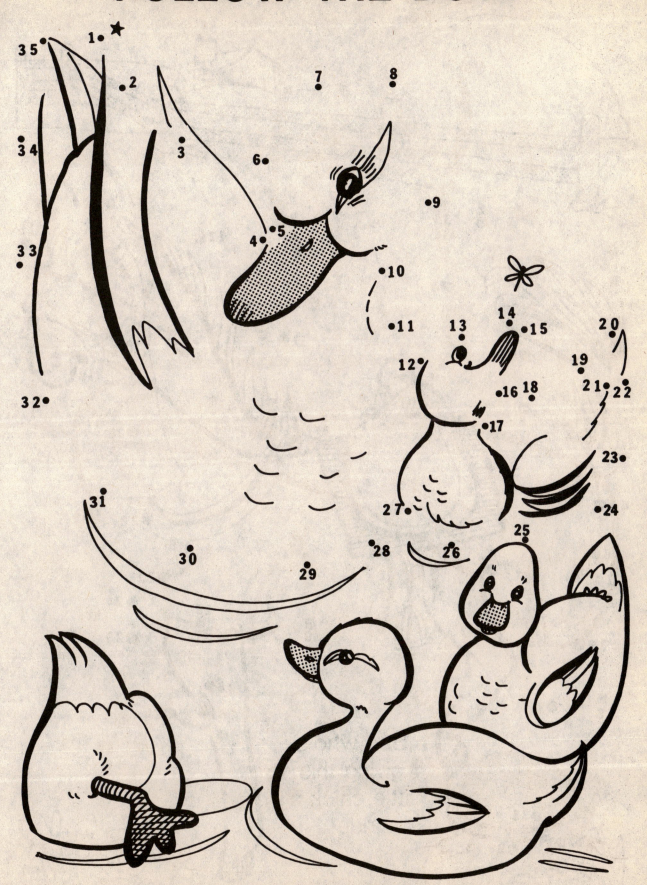

See all the ducks swimming in the pond!

FOLLOW THE DOTS

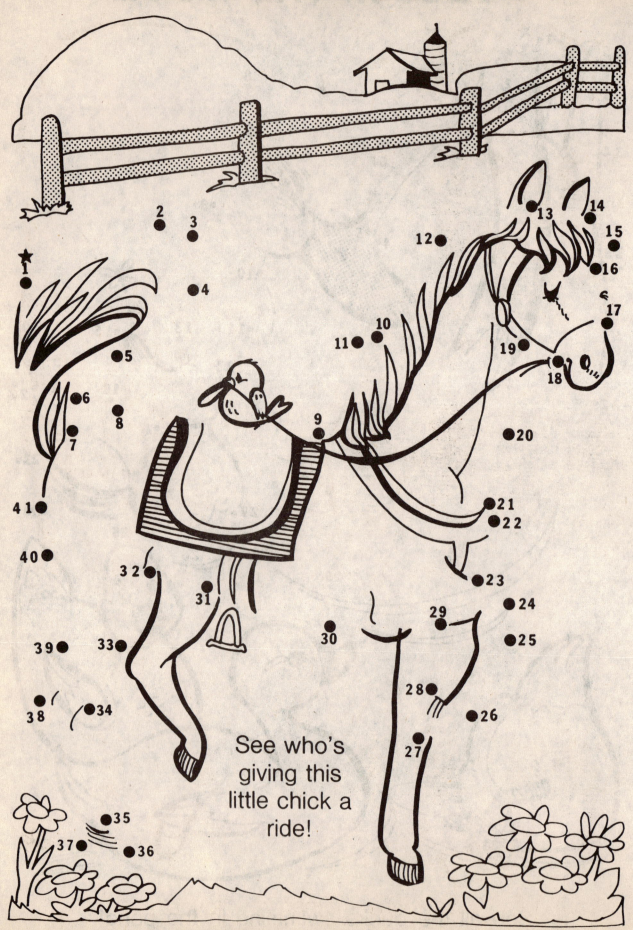

See who's giving this little chick a ride!

FOLLOW THE DOTS

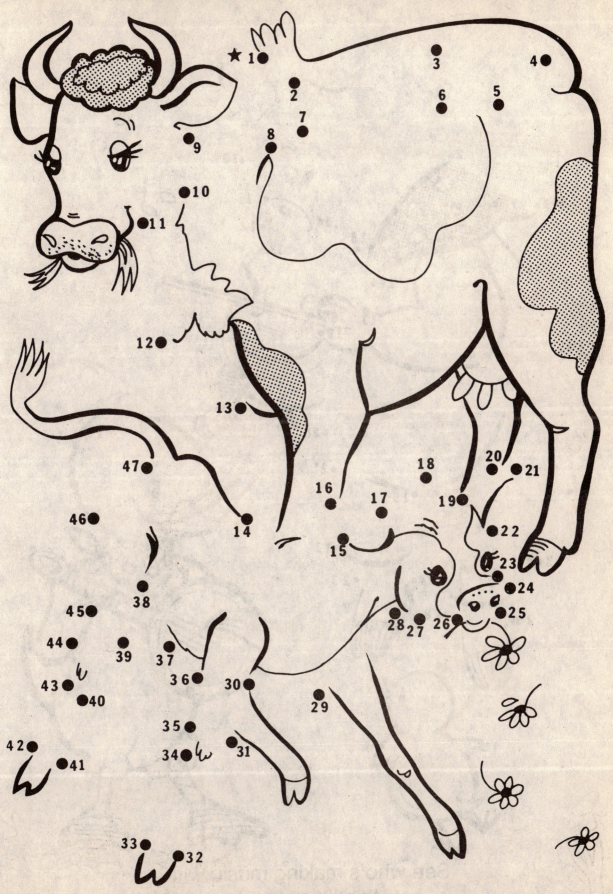

See who mother cow loves!

FOLLOW THE DOTS

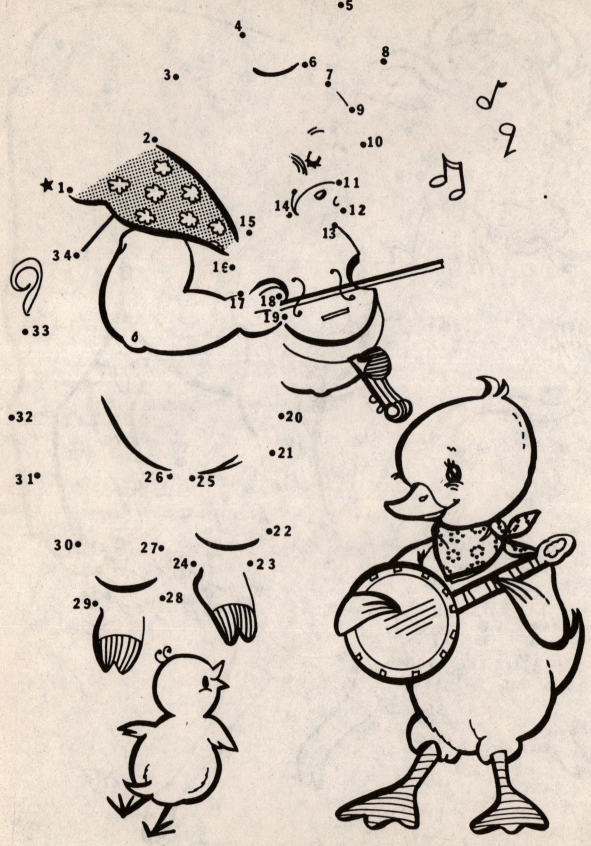

See who's making music with
this little duck!

FOLLOW THE DOTS

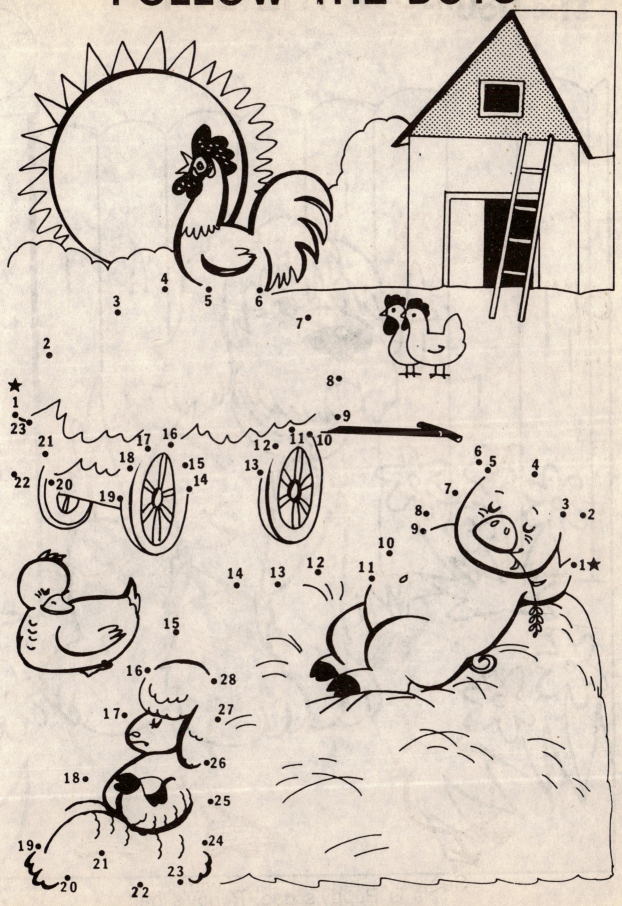

See barnyard friends early in the morning!

The Job

This is Puppy's dad. Puppy's dad
is a guard dog.

Whenever Puppy visits his dad at work, he wishes he had a job of his own. But he's much too young to be a guard dog . . .

. . . and he's too slow to run
at the races.

Puppy doesn't have nearly enough spots
to be a fire dog . . .

. . . and he's hardly husky enough
to pull a sled!

"There must be *something* I can do," Puppy thought.
"But what is it?"

Puppy was still wondering what he could do when a
newspaper suddenly went whizzing through the air.

Quick as a wink, Puppy caught the newspaper before it landed
in the bushes and brought it back to its owner.

"Great catch," the newspaper boy said. "Would you like to help me deliver my papers?"

So now Puppy has the perfect job for him—
newspaper delivery dog!

Lost and Found

There's nothing Puppy loves more . . .

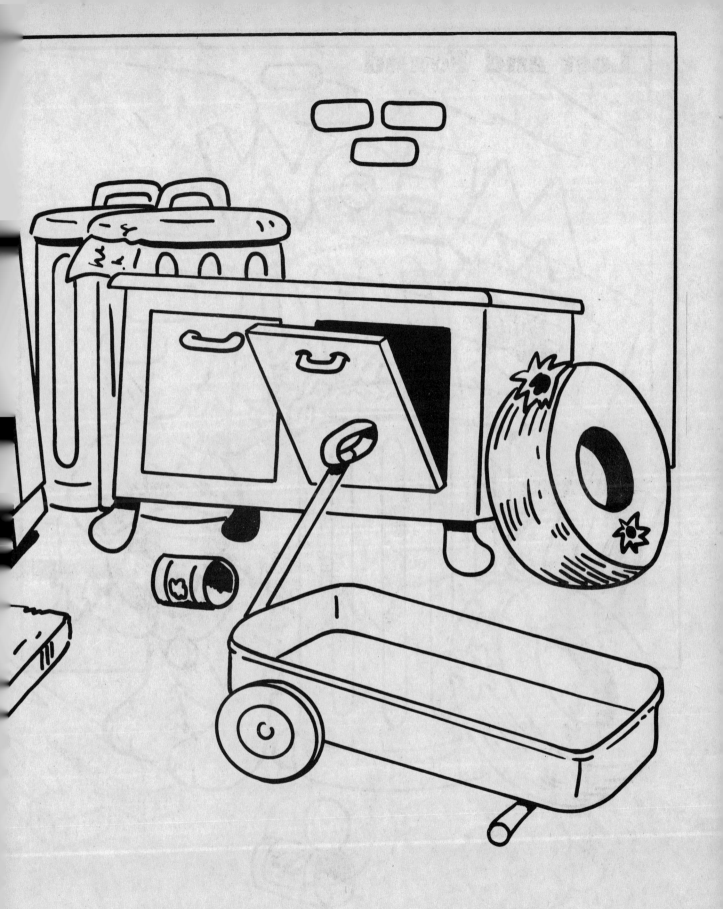

. . . than playing in the junk yard.

"What's that sound?"

"Where is it coming from?"
Puppy wonders.

Puppy looks high . . .

. . . and low, till he finally finds what
he's searching for.

It's a little lost kitten . . .

. . . and a brand-new friend!

Meaner Than Mean

The meanest dog in town lives just down the road from Puppy's house.

"Grrr!" He gives a great growl each
time Puppy walks by.

"Watch out!" Puppy's friends warn. "That dog
is meaner than mean."

"I don't think so," Puppy says. "He looks kind
of sad and lonely to me . . .

... and see how short that rope is. I bet
he never has any fun."

Puppy unties the rope . . .

... and the two dogs go for a long, happy run.

After that, the mean dog doesn't
seem mean at all.

As he waves goodbye to his new friend . . .

. . . he says, "Thanks, Puppy. Please come back and play with me again."

Flying High

"If birds can fly, why can't I?"
Puppy wonders . . .

. . . and he decides to give it a try. Oops! It's not
as easy as it looks.

Maybe if he takes off from a higher place?

No! Puppy still can't fly.

"Tee-hee," the birds chirp. "We could have told him that. Only birds can fly. What a silly Puppy!"

The birds are so busy laughing at poor Puppy that
they knock their nest off its perch.

While the birds flutter about, not sure
what to do . . .

... Puppy leaps off the ground and
catches the nest.

The birds thank Puppy for saving
their nest.

Anyone who can jump that high doesn't
need to know how to fly!

COLOR BY NUMBER

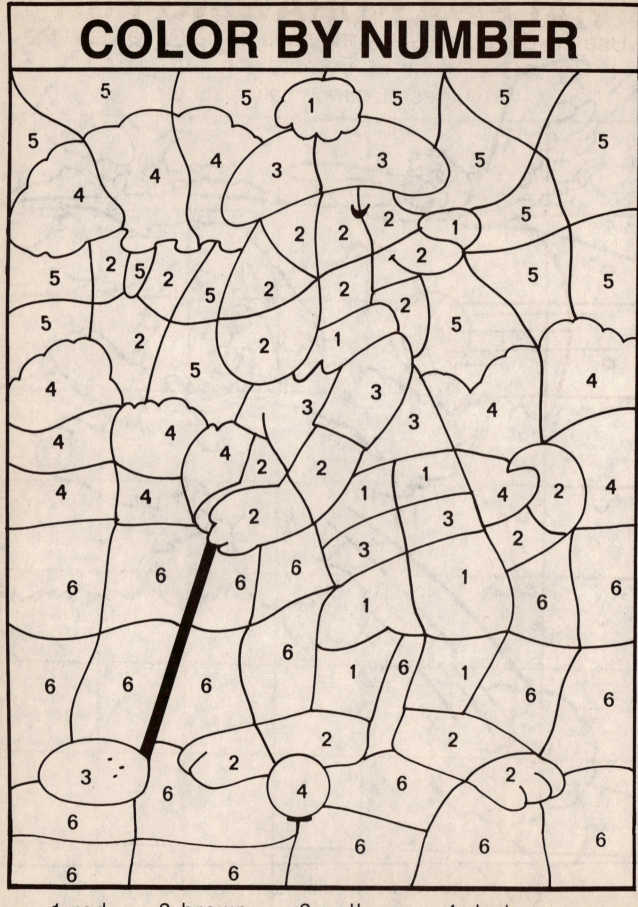

1-red   2-brown   3-yellow   4-dark green
5-blue   6-light green

HALFWAY DRAWING FUN

Use the dotted lines and the squares below to finish the
other half of the St. Bernard dog, the only dog
that rescues mountain climbers.

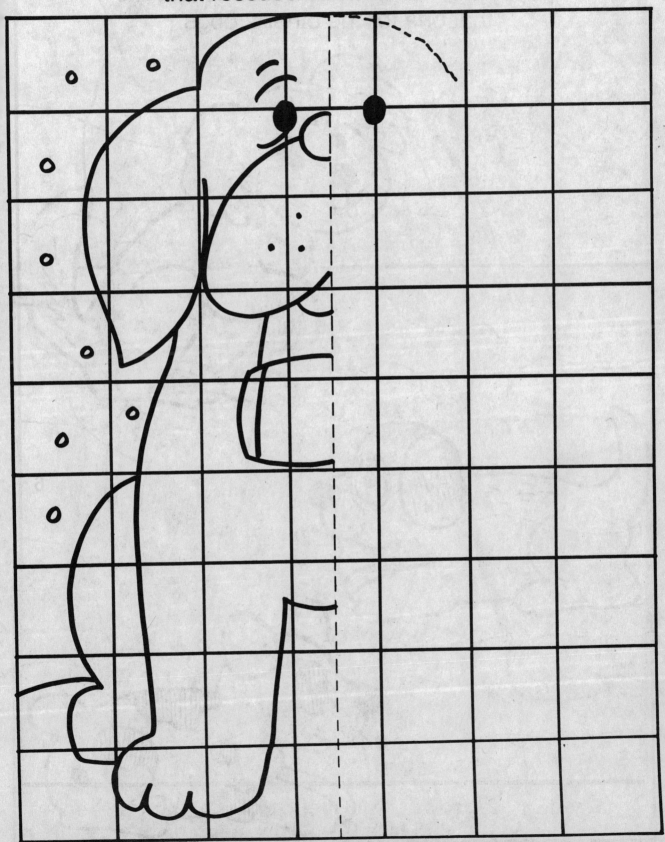

DRAWING FUN

Trace over the dotted lines to draw the puppy's bone. Now draw a bone just like that one for the other 2 dogs.

PUPPY TWINS

Aren't puppies cute?

Can you find the 2 puppies
that look exactly alike?

FOLLOW THE DOTS

Find a furry bicycle rider!

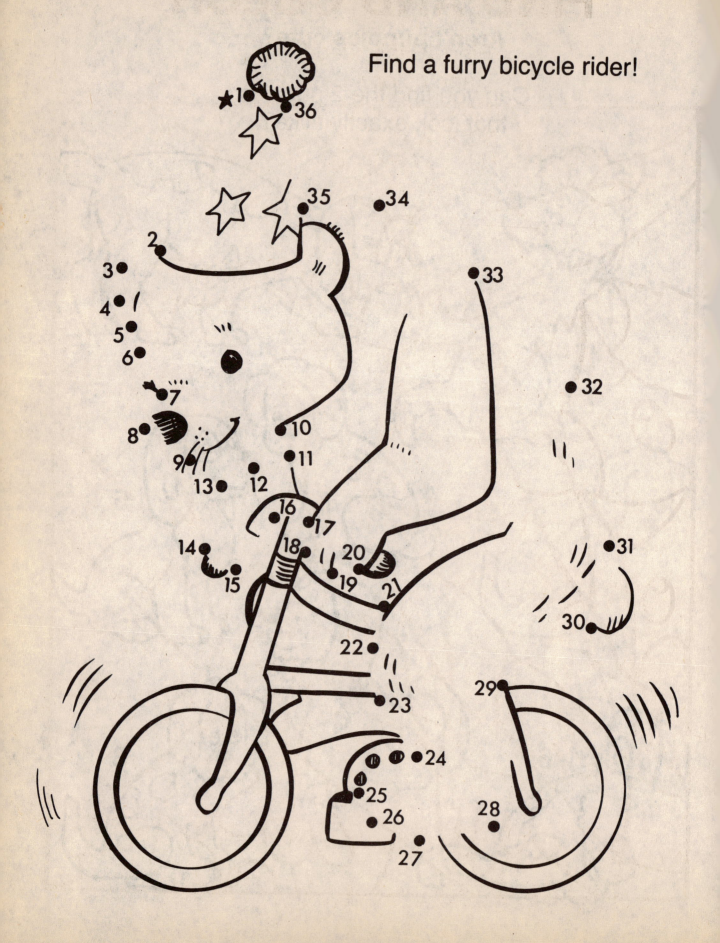

FIND AND COLOR

Find **1** Halloween owl
and color it brown.

FIND AND COLOR

Find **2** winter bears
and color them blue.

MATCH ME!

Match each animal to its shadow in the picture below.

COLOR BY NUMBER

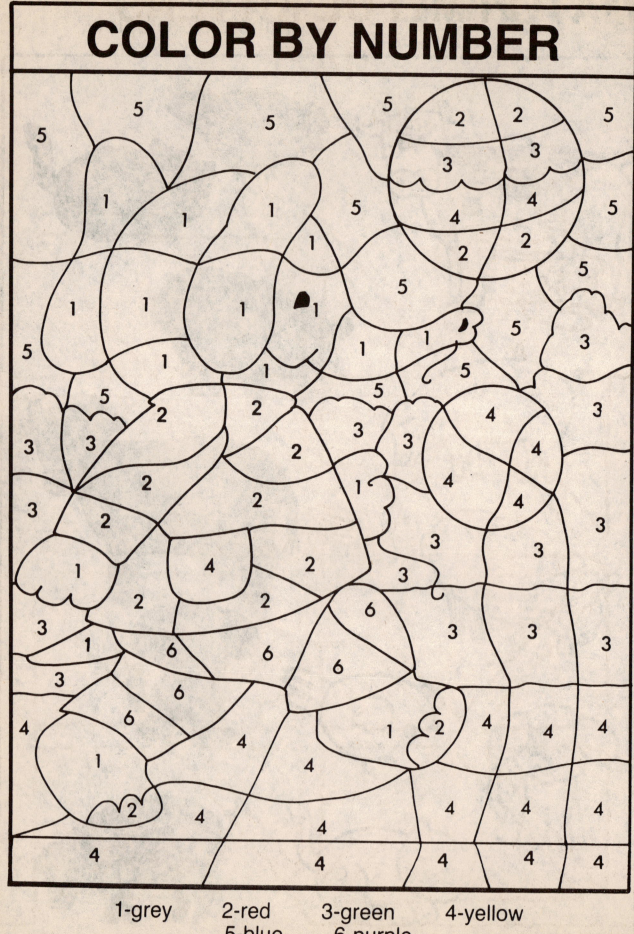

1-grey   2-red   3-green   4-yellow
5-blue   6-purple

PLAYFUL KITTENS
MAZE

Which little kitten gets to play
with the ball of yarn?

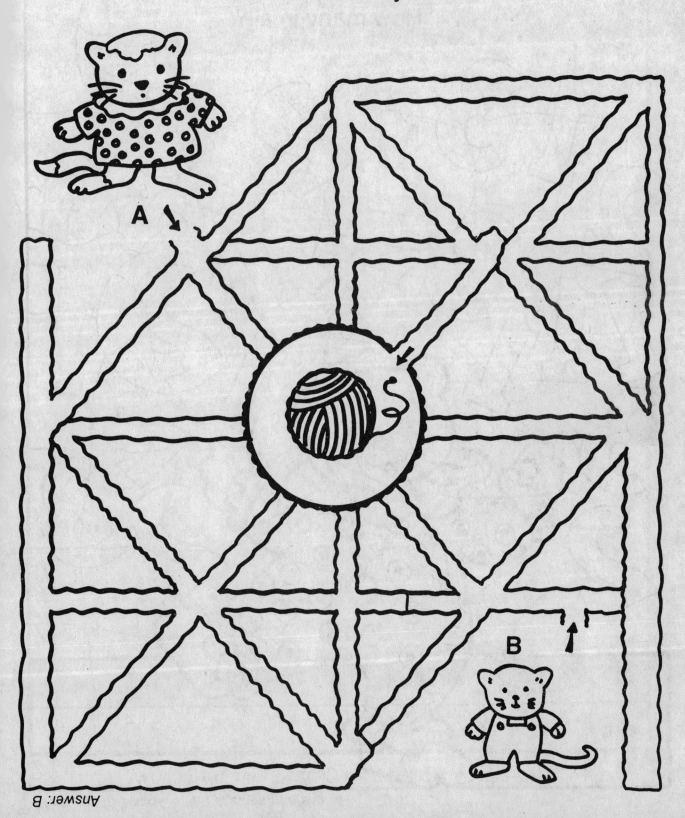

ADDING FUN

How many 1's are there?
How many 2's are there?
How many 3's are there?
How many in all?

COLOR BY NUMBER

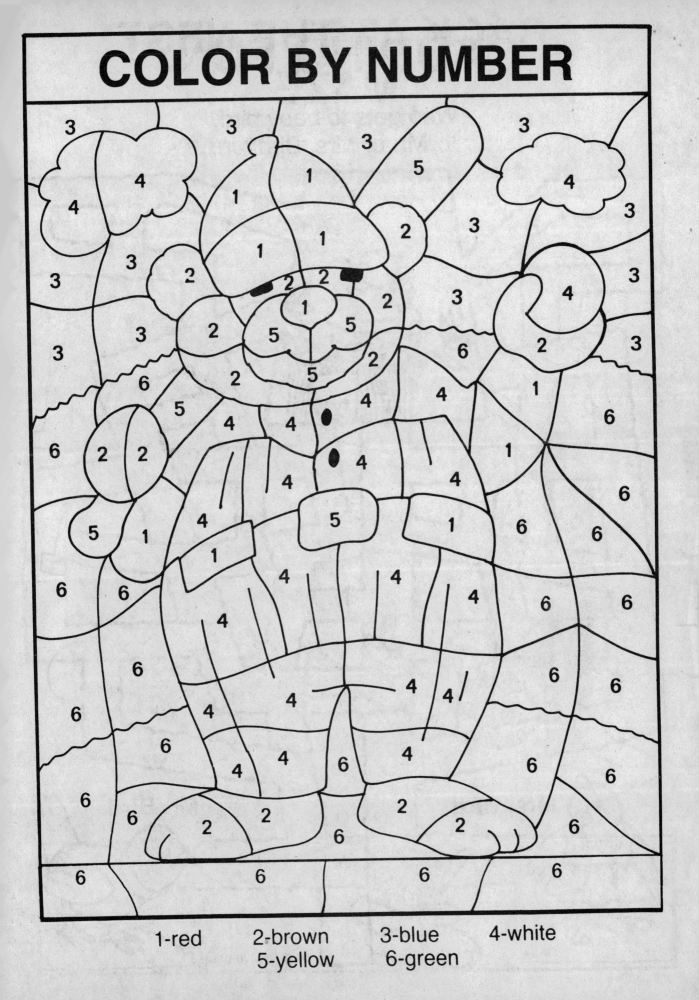

1-red   2-brown   3-blue   4-white
5-yellow   6-green

BACK AT THE NEST MAZE

Who gets to baby bird,
Mr. or Mrs. Bird?

Mrs. Bird

Mr. Bird

Answer: Mr. Bird

FOLLOW THE DOTS

See who is going down the slope!

GOING FISHING

How many fish can you find hiding in the water?

SCRAMBLED ANIMAL FUN

How many cubes of sugar
did Mrs. Elephant
use in her tea?

FOLLOW THE DOTS

What big fellow loves
peanuts best?

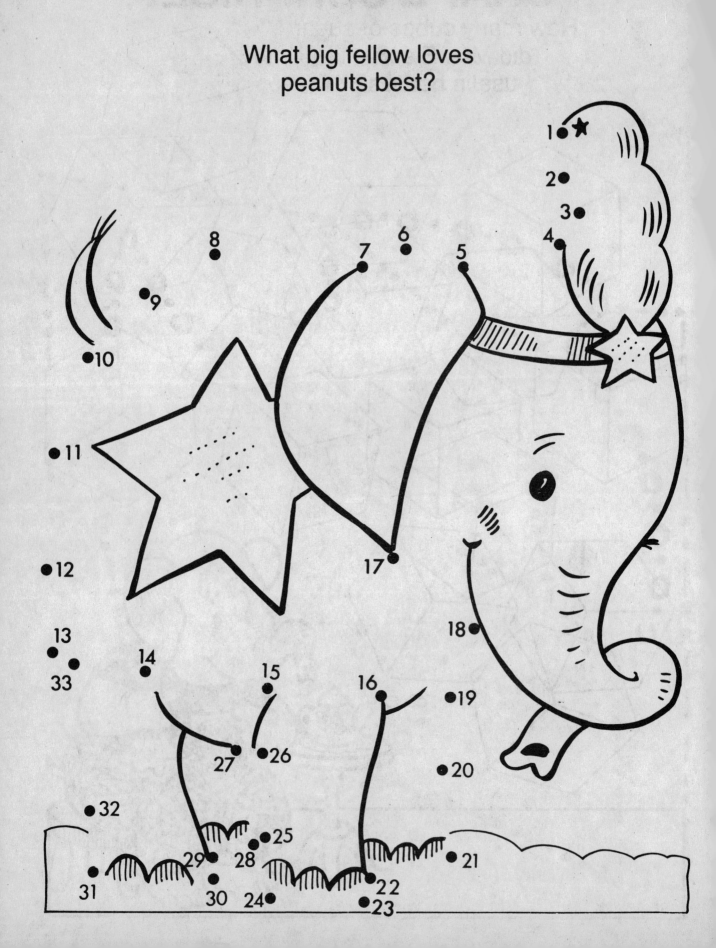